Read wit

Here are some fun activities to prepare your child for reading this book. Take just a few minutes to help your child master new words and reading skills.

Rhyming: Say a word and ask your child to say one that has the same ending sound. For example, you say "day," and your child might say "play."

look   mad   see   get

Sight words: Say each of these words aloud, and help your child find the word in this book. Let your child color in a star beside each word he or she reads.

☆ watch ☆ touch ☆ sorry ☆ forgive ☆ clothes

To, With and By: This technique introduces words into your child's ears first. Then it helps your child to match the words he or she hears to the print on the page.

To: Read the entire story out loud *to* your child. Run your finger under the words as you say them at a normal speed.

With: Read the same story two times *with* your child. Don't slow down, and make sure your child is looking at the words while you read.

By: Let your child read the story *by* himself or herself. Help fix any mistakes.

Have your child read this story for the next several days until it sounds great and is practically memorized.

Dedicated to
Rebecca Wilber

Faith Kids® is an imprint of
Cook Communications Ministries, Colorado Springs, CO 80918
Cook Communications, Paris, Ontario
Kingsway Communictions, Eastbourne, England

What Digby Dug Up
© 2002 by Cook Communications Ministries

First Printing, 2002
Printed in Canada
1 2 3 4 5 6 7 8 9 10 Printing/Year 06 05 04 03 02

Editor: Susan Martins Miller
Cover Design: Big Mouth Bass Design, Inc.
Cover Illustration: Steven Brite
Interior Design: Big Mouth Bass Design, Inc.
Interior Production: Big Mouth Bass Design, Inc.

Unless otherwise noted, Scripture quotations are taken from the Holy Bible: New International Reader's Version®. Copyright © 1998 by International Bible Society. Used by permission of Zondervan Publishing House. All rights reserved.

Library of Congress Cataloging-in-Publication Data

Wilber, Peggy M.
      What Digby dug up / written by Peggy Wilber ; illustrations by Steven Brite.
        p. cm.
      Summary; Hammer's watch is lost and he angrily accuses his brother of taking it, but when the watch turns up they are able to apologize and forgive each other.
      ISBN 0-7814-3724-5
      [1. Lost and found possessions—Fiction 2. Brothers—Fiction. 3. Forgiveness—Fiction. 4. Christian life—Fiction.] I. Brite, Steven, ill. II. Title.

PZ7.W6399 Wh 2002
[E]—dc21

2001023870

GOD PRINTS

What Digby Dug Up

Written by Peggy Wilber
Illustrations by Steven Brite

Equipping Kids for Life!
faithkids.com

"Where is my new watch?"
asked Hammer.
"It was on my desk, but I don't see it."
"Herbie," he yelled,
"did you touch my watch?"

"I don't know where it is,"
said Herbie. "Is it on your desk?"
"It's not there, and you took it,"
said Hammer. "I'm going to
tell Mom."

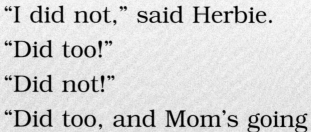

"I did not," said Herbie.
"Did too!"
"Did not!"
"Did too, and Mom's going
to be mad," said Hammer.

"What's the matter?" asked Mom.
"Herbie took my watch,"
said Hammer.

"I touched it," said Herbie,
"but I didn't take it."
"Well, where did it go?"
asked Hammer.
"A watch can't just fly away!"
"Hammer," said Mom,
"maybe you left it outside.
Go and look, please."

Hammer said, "If I don't find my watch soon, you'll have to get a new one for me."

"I'm sorry I touched your
watch, Hammer. Can I help
you look?" asked Herbie.
"No," said Hammer.
"You lost it, and I'm mad."

"Did you touch Hammer's
watch today?" asked Mom.
"Yes, but I didn't take it,"
said Herbie, "and I'm very sorry."

Mom said, "Let's ask God to help Hammer find it. I think you should look for the watch, too." "OK," said Herbie.

"Hi, Herbie," said Pris.
"Hammer is mad at you!"
"I know," said Herbie.
"I said I was sorry, but he
didn't forgive me."

"I hope he finds his watch," Pris said.

"I do too," said Herbie.

"See you soon, Pris."

"Hi, Slink," said Herbie.
"You don't know where
Hammer's watch is, do you?
It's a good thing that animals
don't steal watches!"

"Hey, Herbie," said PJ.

"Hammer has no time for you."

"Get it? He has no time..."

"I get it," said Herbie.

"Did you throw his watch out
the window?" asked PJ.
"Why would I do that?" asked Herbie.
"To see time fly," said PJ. "Get it?"
"I get it," said Herbie. "Good-bye, PJ."

"Digby, it's too bad you don't know where Hammer's watch is," said Herbie.

"I want to find it before
I'm out of time!"

"Did you find your watch, Hammer?" asked Mom.

"No, and I'm mad. Herbie's going to
buy me a new one!" said Hammer.
"Maybe Herbie didn't take your watch.
Maybe it's in your dirty clothes,"
said Mom. "I will look."
"Maybe it's in the garage," said Herbie.
"I will check."

"I'm sorry, Hammer," said Mom.
"It wasn't in your dirty clothes."

"It wasn't in the garage,"
said Herbie.

"Your watch!" said Mom.

"My watch!" said Hammer.

"Your watch!" said Herbie.

"Woof!" barked Digby.

"Good job, Digby,"
they all said together.

"Herbie didn't
take your watch,"
said Mom.

"I'm sorry, Herbie," said Hammer. "I'm sorry for thinking that you took my watch."

"I forgive you, Hammer," said Herbie. "I'm glad you got your watch back. I am sorry I touched it. Next time, I will ask you first."

"Has anyone seen my necklace?" asked Mom. "I can't find it."

Godprint: Forgiveness

When someone hurts you, you don't have to stay angry. Because God forgives us, we can forgive others.

Colossians 3:13
Put up with each other. Forgive the things you are holding against one another. Forgive, just as the Lord forgave you.